My Journey From Darkness Into Light

My Journey From Darkness Into Light

A Testimony

by
Christopher Scott

Epigraph Books
Rhinebeck, New York

My Journey From Darkness Into Light: A Testimony © 2016 by Christopher Scott

All rights reserved. No part of this book may be used or reproduced in any manner without written permission from the author except in reviews and critical articles. Contact the publisher for information.

ISBN: 978-1-944037-30-7

Epigraph Books
22 East Market Street, Suite 304
Rhinebeck, NY 12572

Printed in the United States of America

Introduction

The story that you are about to read is true. Some of the names have been changed for privacy reasons and by the request of the people involved. As a child I experienced many things that were frightening and really had no logical explanation. I had many horrible nightmares throughout my childhood. It would be accurate to say that the nightmares were night terrors. Many of them seemed very real, others were just bad dreams. As I grew older the dreams changed some. Many dreams were beautiful but the nightmares would return.

I'm a born again Christian. I was raised Catholic. Later in my life I walked away from the church. I always believed in God. I just lost faith in the church and in some of the people. I didn't like the way they treated me. I didn't really understand who God really is. I used to think: *Is he my Big daddy? What does he look like? Should I be afraid of him? Maybe he looks like Santa Claus.* These are some of the questions and ideas that I had as a child growing up. I started to experience God. He sometimes would speak to me in my dreams and sometimes when I was awake.

After one of my night terrors, I would hear a voice in my bedroom. He would soothe me. He would say: "Christopher its ok goes back to sleep." I remember talking with him and crying, telling him how scared I was.

"Who are you?" I asked.

"It's God", he answered in a sweet gentle voice. I would usually drift off to sleep again without any dreams. There were many times he would *visit* me. The visits were peaceful and wonderful. I never saw a figure or a person but I did see a light. It was always when my eyes were shut.

There is a dark to all of this. There is always the dark side. Let's call it Satan, the sum of all evil. I have seen him in my night terrors. There was an entity that would haunt me in my dreams. I would call it a demon. It is a mystery as to why this thing would haunt me. It made no sense to me. I remember a little of what it looked like. It was reddish colored and short. It had I's own agenda, to show me hell. That is what I believe. Maybe God in his infinite wisdom

Introduction

let this demon do this. Years later when I was in my thirties I wanted to not believe in hell. Jesus showed it to. I was convinced that it is a real place.

You the reader should take this story seriously. It doesn't matter what religion you are. You need to be saved. Jesus loves you and wants to save your soul. He is the key to eternal life. He is God the son. He is part of the Holy Trinity, Father Son and Holy Spirit.

Chapter 1

This is my testimony of my pre-birth experience. It's something that I'll never forget. Before I was born into this world I remember seeing a man sitting on a chair or throne. He wasn't just any man. There was this brilliant bright light around him. I was standing in front of him. Another person said "Look it's the Lord, isn't he beautiful?, I looked up and saw him and thought, "Yes he is." I saw his bright throne with others in his presence. I do remember how wonderful it was to be there. It was a beautiful place.

Then I remember being in the womb surrounded by water. He then spoke to me.

"Hello Christopher, it's God. You are going to be born now."

I reached out to touch his beautiful bright face.

"Nice Christopher", he said.

That's all that I remember. It's been written in the bible in Jeremiah 1-5,

"Before I formed thee in the belly I knew thee." So, He knew me before he created me. I've drawn a picture of what I saw. It doesn't do him justice but it's the best that I can do. Later on when he spoke to me he commented on it. "It's not quite what I look like but it's an interesting rendition.

Sometimes at night when I close my eyes I can see a light. I know that it's him watching over me. During prayer sometimes the light seems to grow brighter. Then I usually fall asleep soon after.

* * *

This is my testimoy of my experience in that place called hell. Why I was there God himself knows. My experience in this awful place is something that I will never forget. It's part of who I am. As you read this please keep in mind that you need to make sure that you are right with God, and that you've repented all of your sins. This is a real place. It was not just a nightmare. I believe that I was experiencing this for a reason that I will explain later in the next part of my testimony. When I was a child living in West Haven, Connecticut, is when I was brought back there. I was just a child; it didn't make sense to me. I was four going on five when I had this experience repeatedly but in

Chapter 1

different scenarios. These were not dreams; no they were like night terrors. It wasn't in black and white like my dreams are. I know the difference of *bad dreams* and what I went through. I remember we lived in a small but comfortable house. I also had this happen when we moved to Trumbull. This was before I truly accepted Jesus. It has also happened in 2006.

The first *experience* I recall is being in this dark place with walls that seemed endless. There was a floor but it lead nowhere just like the endless wall that had portals. On the other side of this wall were people, many people that were moaning. They were packed together in this one dark place. I do recall seeing *flames* on the other side through the portals. They were being tormented on the other side. I could hear their cries. This *demon* that was standing next to me was the one who also brought me there. I don't recall exactly what he looked like, but I do remember him being rather large.

He asked me, "How do you like this?"

I responded, "No, no." I was so frightened and wondering *What was really on the other side.*

"Get in there," he said. The next momenet he grabbed and threw me through one of the portals. As I'm writing this it's coming back to me. I did wake up crying and I know that I was screaming. My mother came in at one point to comfort me. Before I drifted off I heard a soothing voice. My mother had already gone to bed. I closed my eyes and saw a light as well. The voice was talking to me telling me that everything is ok.

"Go to sleep Christopher it's ok," is what he said. Today I realized who it was, it was the Lord. The Holy Spirit was with me. I felt his presence.

* * *

The second experience that I had went as follows: I was with other people in a dark place with fire burning down below. Others and I were walking on this dark ground. Someone cried out, "Oh my God we're in hell!" There were demons in front of us, one was laughing, at what I don't know. I remember the ounds of people crying out in fear. Hell is a large place with many different parts to it. I can only recall this much. I'm not sure how much more I can talk about this. Maybe it's a blessing that I can't recall any more without hypnosis.

***

Chapter 1

The next one is the most frightening. I saw Satan himself. I'll never forget what he looks like. He is a beast as described in the bible. His demons and spirits are many. I actually drew a picture of what I recall and I shared it with a friend. I prayed to God to help me get this whole experience into the light and to give me courage and strength. My friend Andy saw it and was surprised at it. We went about our work. Later that day he approached me. "Chris, I got to talk with you. I just had the weirdest experience. I think it was the Holy Spirit. He said that I should fold up what you drew into a cross and then burn it. Also he wants you to read the 23rd psalm."

I was amazed and questioned if he ever heard his voice before, and He did when he was younger. I did exactly that and I really felt that God was with me, it was wonderful. He truly is an awesome God and I love him more and more each day. Andy said that he'd fold it up and burn it when he got home. Later he told me that he did.

There is more to this unfortunately but true. There was a demon that would haunt me when I lived in West Haven. It was something that I will always remember. Satan told me that I used to serve him. I know that I was on the wrong path in 2006; Jesus was trying to warn me. This was confirmed through prayer later on. God knows that I needed to change I was headed for destruction. I'm learning how cunning and riley Satan can be. I say to You who is reading this, if you're not saved you must change the path that you're on. God loves you so much. God didn't create hell for us, it's meant for Satan and his angels. God wants us to spend eternity with him. John 3:16 is a great message: "For God so loved the world that he gave his only begotten son, so that whoever believes in him shall not perish but have everlasting life. For God did not send his son to condemn the world; but to save the world through him."

* * *

In June 2008 I was praying very deeply. I heard a voice and saw a light with my eyes closed. I heard a voice that sounded as if it were coming from a tunnel up above me.

"Hello Christopher it's the Lord."

"Oh God, I want to see your face," I said. It was so strange. I saw a white face but it was non descriptive. Also felt someone or many touching my arms as if they were trying to sooth me. My eyes were still closed. His voice changed after I commented on how different he sounded, I did remember him speaking to me as a child when I lived

Chapter 1

in West Haven.

"Lord your voice ssounds different to me."

It sounded different after that as if a great friend was standing next to me and talking.

"You must know about my affair with Belinda, I'm so sorry."

"Yes I do. If you had chosen to be with her she would have broken your heart. She has cancer."

Shocked to hear this, I wanted to cry. She certainly didn't reveal that information to me.

"That is awful," I replied.

I walked into the bedroom trying not to awaken Cheri. I sat on the edge of the bed.

"I created you Christopher, I'm your mother and your father," he sad to me. I had my computer on and my screen saver was a picture of a beautiful woman.

"Lord I asked is this ok with you that I have this up?"

"It's ok with me if it's ok with you?" he answered. I tried to go back to sleep and I did lie down next to Cheri who was sound asleep still.

"I want to sleep," I said. I had slept a total of 4 hours until I woke up around 4:15am.

"Come on sleep," he said.

"Can't sleep. Can't shut off my mind and relax," I responded. I felt like he was getting impatient with me.

"Oh Christopher I knew when I created you that you would be a restless one."

"It's about time that we talked, I love you so much that it breaks my heart," He said.

"I love you too that much."

"Why did you marry her for?" he asked.

"Because I love her," I answered. "Should I try to work things out with her?"

"Yes."

"Lord I want to ask you something."

"Yes what?"

"Is Ashley my daughter?"

"Yes she is," he replied.

That made me feel good, at least I know the truth I thought to myself.

He knows us better than we know ourselves. In the book of Jeremiah Chapter 1:4 he tells Jeremiah, "Before I formed you in the womb I knew you."

"I want to tell everyone at work about this."

"Will you turn around before I turn into a rabbit?"

I started to laugh and said that I

Chapter 1

would and I did turn around back home. I realized that it was about 5:00am and I needed to get ready for work. I told Cheri about what happened and her reaction was, "Chris you got to stop this."

"Stop what," I replied, "I'm just telling you what happened."

She gruntingly went back to sleep. I've heard his wonderful voice before I was so happy to hear it again.

"Lord I have a question."

"Yes."

"I feel as though that I lived another life."

"Yes you were Christopher Koegel, you flew a large jet in the German Luftwaffe, and you crashed your plane. You ate a dead man's finger after you cut it off with a hack saw. You died in 1947."

"Oh no that was pretty sick of me wasn't it." I felt awful.

"Well yes. I had to send you to hell Chris."

"How many times have I been there?"

"Four times," he answered.

I thought to myself it's no wonder why I was so fascinated with World War Two and Nazi Germany. I was especially interested in German uniforms.

"Lord, am I going to Heaven or hell when I die?"

"It hasn't been decided yet," he answered quietly.

"When am I going to die?"

This answer was hard to take and I'm sort of sorry that I asked that question because I don't want to know the hour nor the day when this happens.

"In your fifties," he answered.

I got up out of bed again and went into the kitchen. I wanted to tell everyone about this conversation so I started walking down the road barefooted at 5:15am.

"Where are you going?" the Lord asked me.

I looked around for my wallet and realized that I couldn't find it. That means I couldn't get to work. I called in sick for the morning. I somehow found my wallet an hour later. I got into my car and left the house figuring that I didn't want to teal with Cheri who was probably in a bad mood because of my waking her up. As I was driving to Poughkeepsie I heard his voice again.

"That's an interesting car you have."

"Yes it is, you know I want to pretend that you're sitting next to me."

"I'm always with you," He responded.

"Thank you Lord."

"I was too early to see my therapist at Spectrum so I decided to go to the gym.

Chapter 1

As I went in I remember the lady at the desk greeting me.

I told her that I spoke to the Lord today and life is good. She smiled in repsonse. Later that day I called my brother in law Mark and told him that the Lord had spoken to me. My sister called back later on and had me repeat what I said to her the day before. When I had the demon attach itself to me two days before, I did make weird gestures as if I were shooting a gun at my work place. It was not me. I realized this when I looked into the reflection of my car window. It was not me that I saw but a red face with this wide smile.

I didn't understand what was happening but I knew that I didn't feel right. I wanted to fight this any way that I could. It spoke out of me.

"I'll be back," it said.

"Stop it. Stop it. Jesus make it stop," I yelled as I pounded the steering wheel of my Jeep. I will elaborate more on this later in my testimony.

I asked the Lord about a strange dream that I had when I was 14 years old. It was so real it didn't seem like a dream. One morning back when we lived in Trumbull Connecticut I got out of bed around 3:30 AM. I though that I heard someone at the front door. I got up thinking *what the hell?*

Were there kids playing games with me?

No way, I thought. Who was at the front door at this late hour?

I opened the door and saw someone dressed in a dark suit. This *person* was trying to talk to me. That's all I remembered. At first I thought that it was someone wearing a space suit. That must have been a false memory. I asked the Lord about that, he replied:

"That was me Christopher." It sort of made sense to me, as I know that the Lord can appear to us in different ways. I was sure that I wasn't just dreaming this whole thing. If it was truly the Lord, it was a weird memory. I believe that it was God. He does appear to us in different ways. Some have spelled roses but didn't see an apparition.

It is said in the bible that "No one who sees me will live."

That explains why I can't say that I know God's true form. I've been told that I've seen him before. It must have been between my past lives. I still have a lot of questions for God. I don't understand our conversation and why would he say that he would turn me into a rabbit if I didn't turn back and go home. I guess that he was joking with me.

So that morning in June 2008 I did turn around and walked back home. I

Chapter 1

remember that I could not find my wallet. I called my dispatcher and told him that I cannot do my morning run. I got in the car after finding my wallet and went to the gym. I walked the track upstairs. The weirdest thing happened, I actually hard my mother speak to me. She said she was sorry for being abusive to me. I told her it was okay.

I did leave the gym and went to my counselor's office. I tried to get in to see her but she was not available. I did go to work that morning. And my sister Tina called me. I told her about what happened on Wednesday with the demonic spirit. They misunderstood me and thought that I said that I had a gun with me. This was not true; I would never carry a gun to school. They did call Cheri and we had a three-way conversation. Later that afternoon Cheri came and got me from work. My father, my sister Tina, and Markel showed up at the counselor's office. I told them all what happened on Wednesday. My dad and my sister decided to have me committed to a hospital. So for the next 12 days I went to a hospital in Putnam County.

I saw this figure in a dream when I was fourteen years old. It seemed so real.

Chapter 2

March 15, 2011

I was on my bus when I received the first text message from Michelle. She told me that she heard a raspy voice talk to her at the house earlier. It wanted to take the letter that I showed her about God and shove it up her ass. I was shocked when I heard this. She told me that she felt a spirit enter her at work. She prayed and it left her.

I suggested having the house blessed. The spirit said that, "It wasn't a good idea."

I knew then what we were dealing with wasn't good. I was very concerned so I called Helen who contacted Pastor Pat from Newburgh.

We all agreed to meet in Gardiner then follow me to my house. I was very uneasy and my thoughts were racing.

What the hell is going on I thought, *What are we dealing with?* As I crossed the mid-Hudson bridge I heard someone or something say to me; "Why don't you just jump off and end it all?"

"No I won't," I replied.

I met Helen in Gardiner and Pat showed up soon afterward. They followed me back to my house. After we arrived Helen started blowing her *shofar* outside the house. We all went inside and started talking about the weird activity. I told them about Michelle's encounter with the demonic spirit in her room downstairs. Helen went downstairs and suddenly screamed: "Oh my God I can't breathe it's down here!"

"Are you ok?" we both asked.

Pat and I looked at each other in horror as then hurried down the stairs. As we came to the door that leads to the room we both started praying. Helen joined in.

"In the name of Jesus I command you to get out of this house!" Pat said. I was on my knees at this point. Pat then took some anointing oil and made a sign of the cross above the doorway.

"It's gone," he said quietly

That same afternoon I lay down on the bed downstairs and that's when things got really weird. I heard someone say to me: "Christopher, I'll be back you used to serve me." It had a raspy tone and I didn't understand what was going on. I caught a

Chapter 2

glimpse of a face but couldn't distinguish who it was.

I had a bad feeling about this and thought that it may be old Satan himself. I somehow knew that voice. I sat up with eyes wide open.

"I don't think so get out of here in the name of Jesus you son of a bitch."

I realized what I said and I later asked for forgiveness from God.

I had a quick vision of me wearing a military uniform

I could almost hear the Horst Wessel Lied playing in my head. This was known as the German National Socialist Anthem. It was as if a chorus was singing this. I still have a hard time understanding this.

I understand now what God had revealed to me in 2008. As I commanded the Devil to get out and stay out Michelle came into the room.

"What's going on? You're scaring me."

"It's starting to make sense now." I replied. "The Holy spirit told me who I was in a former life. I was Christopher Koegel. I flew a big jet in the German Luftwaffe in world war two. I crashed my plane. I was so hungry that I ate a dead man's finger after I cut it off with a hack saw. I died in 1947."

Thursday came and it was St. Patrick's Day. I had an early supper with some friends in Poughkeepsie. I went home afterward. My friend Helen had invited me over her house for dinner so I went. Her friend John was there and we all discussed Jesus and the bible in general,

That evening I did not sleep well at all. I felt a presence in the bedroom and heard the Holy Spirit speak to me. He said to me: "Feel my spirit, relax you should be asleep soon."

I surely did and I saw his light with my eyes closed. I tried to sleep but couldn't settle down. I got up and took an aspirin. I got back into bed and out of frustration I cried out, "It's hard being me!"

"I know," he replied.

I finally got up and went to work. For some reason I had Satan on my mind and couldn't shake the image of him from my mind. Later on that morning I decided to draw a picture of what I thought that he looked like. I shared it with a coworker Andy.

He told me that a spirit told him to fold the picture into a cross and burn it. We both felt a presence in our office. It must have been the Holy Spirit. Andy told me of this and I got a frightened.

Andy said, "He wants you to read the 23rd Psalm and relax not to worry anymore."

So I did and felt as though God was talking to me through the scriptures.

Chapter 2

* * *

On March 18th I went to sing at Cabaret night. This is an annual show that the local theater company puts on. I'll never forget that night. After I sang the song "Cabaret" I sat in the audience. After everyone was finished with their applause, I distinctly heard another audience praising me. I heard them over my shoulder as if it were coming from another dimension. I realized that the voices I heard were my mother's, Forest's, Grandma Helga, Grandpa Tony and Grandma Ruie. There may have been others.

My Grandpa Tony praised me. It was weird to say the least. In a way I felt wonderful knowing that I wasn't alone. After the show was over Helen and I came back to my house and watched movies she was very upset with her life and how heartbroken she was over her husband leaving. I decided to pray at my alter, she joined in. I sang and prayed. I could feel the presence of the Holy Spirit.

I remember how depressed that she was. My girlfriend Michelle came home and went downstairs. I went downstairs spoke to her for a few minutes, explaining that I had to drive Helen home. The ride was quiet except for what I heard a voice deep inside me say: "Do not spend too much time there."

My thoughts were starting to race. Who is this I thought, it must be the Holy Spirit. As we entered her house I noticed her friend Mark and her daughter were hanging out in the living room watching television. I felt a weird presence in the house, and quickly went to the bathroom. After using the bathroom I became frightened. I prayed quietly to God for protection. Helen turned on her computer and started searching for something. "I just want to be with the Lord" she said. "I know you do," I responded.

'You know some day there will be aliens coming to help us", I said. I don't know why I said that. I know very little about that subject and only from what I've read in the media.

She then decided to give communion. I found this a little odd but went along with it. After I ate a morsel of bread and drank the juice, weird things started to happen. I felt different. I hugged Helen said to her: "I am Jesus and I'll be back to take you home with me."

I then looked in the reflection of the kitchen window. It was not my reflection looking back. It was something else. It had bright red eyes and a dark colored face. There were two of these creatures looking back at me. I immediately left and drove away in my car. As I approached the turn from route

Chapter 2

#207 to 44/55, I felt this stabbing pain in my stomach. I suddenly remembered what God warned me about staying at Helen's house too long. This hurt so badly that I pulled the car over.

"Oh my God, I get it what just happened?" I yelled.

"I'm so sorry God", I cried.

I thought that I had been jumped or possessed by a demon.

I continued driving back to my house in silence. When I arrived home I called Helen and apologized.

"It's ok, that was not you saying those things Chris. "She responded.

'You have something evil in your house. You should contact Pastor Pat," I said.

"Well, I will do that soon." She answered in a weepy voice.

"I'm so sorry", I said.

"Good night Chris call me tomorrow."

I hung up the phone and went to bed. It was after 1:00am.

* * *

March 20, 2011

On Sunday morning during prayer I was allowed to see something very odd. It had been a long and stressful week. There was a demonic spirit in my house which I had to have exorcised out on Tuesday. This is explained in another part of my testimony. My house has been peaceful ever since that weird event. Here it was Sunday morning and before I got out of bed I prayed for strength as I do every day. I knew that I needed it today especially. I sensed something was still up.

During prayer I was given a bird's view of a man being nailed to a cross. I guess that it was Jesus.

"You do understand the sacrifice that had to be made," a male voice told me.

"Yes I do," I responded.

Later that morning I went to church. I sat in the front pew like I always do. A woman sat next to me. She was probably in hr 40s with curly hair and attactive. At the end of the service she introduced herself to me as Pam. When the service ended I caught up with my pastor and we prayed in his office. That is when I saw these greenish eyes looking back at me; my eyes were closed at this point. I didn't understand what I saw, I did gasp, "Oh God help me."

It then went away. As I left his office I started to head toward the church hall. I heard a voice say, "Don't go in there."

What? I thought. "Don't follow her Chris, she is from the enemy. Wait in the

Chapter 2

church until Michelle comes to get you," the voice said. I stayed in the church until she arrived to pick me up. I never saw that woman again. That was very creepy.

Chapter 3

August 2011

I was standing on the battlefield at Pennsic watching everyone gather up. This is a medieval event which I attend annually.

I heard Satan speak to me. I knew it was him, I heard him speak to me at my home back in March .He said that I used to *serve* him. This could be interpreted as before I was saved. It was a beautiful warm afternoon at that medieval event called Pennsic.

"You know I wasn't going to hurt Michelle, I was only messing with her."

"I see," was my response as I tried not to draw attention to myself.

"You know sometimes I eat rabbits for breakfast they're very good," He said to me. I started to feel uneasy being in the battlefield where many spectators were watching the event.

"Uh I see" was my response.

Chapter 3

"I'll be around," he said. "But I know your house is protected. Talk with you later Christopher Koegel."

"I'm done with this conversation in the name of Jesus," I said quietly.

When I came back I had my pastor prayed over me. The enemy is riley and occasionally does put thoughts in my mind and does try to talk with me.

I told some of my friends about what happened. They were surprised to say the least. Every day I get up and say, "Good Morning Lord I love you. May I put on your armor as I go fourth today?"

Before my wife at the time left, I was struggling with the Lord and my faith. I wanted to be closer to him. One night I had a dream so real that it bothered me for a month. I dreamt that I was near this *tunnel*. This tunnel was leading to a place that had fire, with many levels to it. I saw many friends of mine falling through these tunnels into this place. I was with a man witnessing this. This was revealed to me through prayer that I was seeing hell itself.

I know now that I'm on the right path. I've heard the Lord speak to me again.

"Don't be afraid." He said.

One morning I did smell roses, before I went into work. I prayed afterward. I could feel the Holy Spirit with me. It is an amazing thing; then again God is amazing and awesome. I will never understand how the Holy Trinity works. Its ok, I'm not supposed to understand it all.

About a year later I was coming home from work and heard from the dark side again. I'm not sure who it was. This spirit was trying to talk to me .I didn't recognize who it was at first but there was a cold feeling about it.

"Christopher, I'm trying to talk to you." The male voice said, "You are impossible." The voice said. It didn't sound like the Holy Spirit.

"Who are you?" I asked.

"You know who this is." He said in a deep voice. I thought to myself God?, no way it didn't feel right.

"I don't know who you are in Jesus name." I said.

There was no response at first. I started singing a Christian song.

I didn't like what I was feeling.

"God?, I asked what is going on?" I didn't get an answer.

One of the many peculiar things that I've noticed about when I go to this event I feel spiritual energy. There are nights when I have horrific night mares while at this event. I dream of being in a gang and I'm fighting others with knives and guns. There are days

Chapter 3

of peace. I look for that peace when I pray to God. I would go to this event to escape my real life as many others do. I don't go to this event anymore. There have been too many negative encounters that I've had with dark energy, let's call it evil. I've heard demonic spirits and devils talk to me, taunting me to *go have fun. You like that woman that you're staring at go talk to her, you know you want her.* I simply replied NO.

It was revealed to me during prayer one day that I lived in Whales England in a former life many years ago. I didn't ask when. I was also told that I was a Roman soldier. This accounts for three of my past lives, A Welsh many years ago, I lived in the early 1920s, was killed in a bar fight. I must have been reborn soon after and lived as A German. I later joined the German Luftwaffe and trained as bomber pilot in World War 2. My name was Christopher Koegel. I researched this person on the internet. There were two Germans with that same name but no other information was listed.

Chapter 4

Those succubus spirits were here. I know because I felt them. They told me who they were.

"I don't care if you all watch me," I said. "You are not welcome here; get out in the name of Jesus Christ!"

The female sounding voices stopped. These spirits have haunted my dreams also. I saw one in a dream who was trying to seduce me. I'll never forget what she looked like, tall blonde with grayish looking skin. I resisted them and I woke up. I started praying to God for protection. In ancient folk lore they are capable of stealing souls. I won't write any more about them.

* * *

Conversations with the Dead
3/2014

Chapter 4

I've always had an interest in world war two. I recently started collecting replica German uniforms from the era. Prior to this incident I was at a movie theater in Kingston with some friends. Before the movie started I felt as if something or someone was watching me from afar. I looked to my left and saw a shadow figure standing about ten feet away. It was wearing a peaked hat of some kind. That was all I saw. I couldn't figure out who or what it was. It then vanished.

Later on that year I was at work using the bathroom. As I was finishing up I heard a male voice start talking to me.

"Christopher" the voice said.

"Nice uniform you have. You like making fun of me don't you?"

"What?" I answered. "Yes I do. Who are you?"

"I am the Fuhrer", he answered in a thick accent.

"Where are you?" I asked not believing this whole conversation.

"Where do you think I am? I'm in hell."

"I hope the devil goes easy on you Adolf."

I wanted to laugh at all of this but couldn't grasp it all.

"Why did you kill all those Jews?" I asked.

"I hated Jews." He answered.

"I got to go now bye bye." I responded.

I must have opened up some type of doorway with my interest in the war.

He spoke to me a few months later commenting on what I needed to add to the Luftwaffe uniform.

Another spirit said: "Don't listen to him."

I realized that it was my mother. She speaks to me sometimes also.

My Grandpa Delmar has said hello to me and I've also dreamt of him. He passed away in 1983. My Mom died in 1992.

As you are reading this keep this in mind, I do not recommend that anybody talks with the dead. This must be a gift. Having this ability, I'm very careful. This is a dark side to this. The devil also speaks to me. He is riley, sneaky, lies a lot and wants me to follow him. He knows that I'm saved by the blood of Jesus Christ. It is written in the bible; Resist the devil and he will flee. I still struggle with many things. I'm learning to give it to Jesus. I still mess up, I'm a WIP. Work IN Progress.

* * *

7/16/15

I was in the bathroom washing my hands when I heard a man speaking to me in a German accent.

Chapter 4

"You're a good man Christopher. Do you remember Krystal Nacht?" Krystal Nacht meant Night of broken glass. It was an event where the Nazis and several other people threw rocks through the windows of the Jewish shops in Berlin and other cites as well.

"You were there Christopher," he said his voice was coming from a short distance away.

"Who are you?" I asked.

"I am Der Fuhrer," he said.

"Yes you were there and you shot some Jews," he said.

"I don't really remember that," I answered feeling sick to my stomach.

"Yes you did," he repeated.

"Can I call you Adolf?" I asked, not believing what I just heard.

"Yes, I'm Adolf Hitler."

"How do you know what I'm thinking, can you read my mind?"

"Yes I can," he answered.

"Aren't you in Hell?" I asked.

"Yes I am. I'm with the devil, he likes me. He likes you too," he said.

This actually happened early around 8:16AM.

I started praying the Lord's Prayer after hearing that man's voice. This story has no end; it goes on and on until I die. You the reader I want you to know that everything that you have read is true. The devil continues to haunt me. I always tell him to, "Get behind me Satan." The more that I resist him the less he comes around with his demons, devils and succubus spirits.

I always call on Jesus. He is God the son. Aba Father and the Holy Spirit are always there for me even if I don't always hear a voice. May God guide me with his love and grace until I can be with him eternally.

* * *

11/17/15

My wife Michelle heard a loud banging in the garage of our house. This happened one morning about a week ago. My first thought was, *Are one of the cats down there.* That same day I prayed over the situation. I went down into the garage to investigate, since our house has become a haven for paranormal activity. There were neither cats nor anything else that I could find.

I prayed at the alter in the bedroom. The Holy Spirit revealed to me that it was a *demon of rebellion*. This *demon* has been here before. I went into the garage and performed a blessing on the garage. I asked that the guardian angel Michael send his angels

Chapter 4

down to protect our house. The garage has been quiet ever since thank God.

The other night my wife heard a knocking at the downstairs door. I went to investigate, nobody was there. So here we are again another day in my life. I'm beginning to see a pattern with these demons. They seem to show up every few months or so. May God help us all, Amen.

www.ingramcontent.com/pod-product-compliance
Lightning Source LLC
Chambersburg PA
CBHW051720040426
42446CB00008B/973